GOD KEEPS COVENANT

A Thirty-Day Study
on God's Love for Israel

Wendy D. Beckett

GOD KEEPS COVENANT
A Thirty-Day Study on God's Love for Israel
by Wendy D. Beckett

"Reading Wendy Beckett's thirty-day devotional *God Keeps Covenant* has blessed me greatly. Each day contains an important message and an unmistakable call for the Body of Christ. It is a treasure of excellent teaching derived straight from the Bible where God's heart of love for His people is revealed and how we, the church, fit into His plan of Israel's restoration. I highly recommend this devotional to anyone who has a love for God and a desire to discover the richness of His covenant promises."

Markus Ernst
Chairman of the Board, Operation Exodus, Ebenezer Emergency Fund

"The Jewish people occupy a unique place and play out a 'pivotal' role in the unfolding redemptive purposes of God in the earth. Unfortunately, multitudes of devoted Christians have never explored or been taught to understand and appreciate the hundreds of scriptures referencing God's ongoing Covenantal regard for Israel, His chosen people.

This 30-day devotional by Wendy Beckett is an excellent introduction, refresher course, and graduate seminar all rolled into one. It reflects the heart of God Himself, and the heart of one who has engaged these truths in serious study, intercessory prayer and works of mercy over many years. As you read and grow in your understanding of God's unending love for Israel, you will also better comprehend His measureless love for you and yours!"

Gary P. Bergel
President, Intercessors for America

"I found this book to be a prayerfully written thirty-day journey revealing a majestic covenant-keeping God who through ISRAEL has given us Proof of His eternal love.

May we all take this journey and by faith have a greater sense of awe and assurance that we serve this great covenant-keeping God who bought us with His own blood."

Sally N. Fesperman
Cofounder of Christian Training Center, Franklin NC; Derek Prince Ministry board member; Youth Counselor

God Keeps Covenant
A Thirty-Day Study on God's Love for Israel

For ease of readability, I have quoted from the New International Version (NIV) of the Bible, except in a few cases that I have noted as follows:

NKJV – New King James Version
CJB – Complete Jewish Bible

The emphasis in **bold font** is my choice.

Copyright regulations for the NIV require the use of the lower case for pronouns referring to the Lord. However, out of reverence to the Lord and because this is a devotional, I have used upper case, such as "You," "Him," and "His," in the prayers and wherever else possible.

Endnotes are at the back of the book. All other permissions granted.

Jacket illustration by: Paul Clark & Sharon Raymond

Book design by: Brian Sooy & Co.

To the Lord, Jesus, our Messiah and King

To John, my beloved husband and best friend

To our precious family

To the Church and the Jewish people,
whom the Lord loves so dearly

{ CONTENTS }

God Keeps Covenant
A Thirty-Day Study on God's Love for Israel

Introduction

"Maybe that's what the prophets meant!" my mother mused aloud one morning in May of 1948. She and I were making beds as she was considering the significance of the newly formed State of Israel. I was nine years old, growing up in Toronto, Canada, where I already had many Jewish friends. Although I didn't realize it until much later, the Lord would use that single comment by my mother to propel me into a keen interest in what God was doing with the Jewish people and the State of Israel in our day. As I read the Bible I found myself taking words like "Israel," "Zion," or "Jerusalem" literally, as well as seeing them figuratively for individual Christians and the Church as a whole.

So began a lifelong pursuit to understand this vital topic. I never dreamed as a child that decades later, my husband John and I would become immersed in activities supporting this aspect of God's agenda, including a massive effort to bring Jewish people out of the former Soviet Union back to Israel.

So why this devotional study?

There are so many questions among Christians today concerning the Lord's relationship with the Jewish people. What about the Holocaust? Why did God allow such atrocities if the Jews are still His chosen people? What is the Lord's view of the modern State of Israel? Why is much of the Church silent on this whole issue?

Early in the Christian era, opinions hardened on the way God regarded the Jewish people. Negative attitudes toward them developed almost immediately after the apostles' deaths and have held sway throughout most of Christian history.

So I am inviting you to explore this topic with me. My emphasis will be to unfold Scriptures that shed light on God's longstanding devotion to the Jewish people. This study will involve a short daily reading for 30 days.

Many Scriptures give us insight into the Lord's attitude toward those He has called "My people." In fact I've cited more than a hundred. These Scriptures – from both the Old and New Testaments – have not gone out of date. They apply today to Jew and Gentile alike.

In this devotional, I am not presenting a theological argument but telling a love story. The Father in heaven has chosen a people for Himself for purposes that are still not fully complete.

As we find with any specific passages of Scripture, some seem logical, but many require the Lord's light to shine on them. I encourage you to read these Scriptures **slowly and prayerfully**, allowing the depth of their meaning to penetrate deeply into your heart. I trust you'll find, as I have, the enormity of God's love toward these people He has called His own.

A Love Story

"His love endures forever." (PSALM 118:2)

*"…give thanks to the Lord for **his unfailing love.**"*
(PSALM 107:8, 15, 21, 31)

*"The Lord your God has chosen you …to be his people, his treasured possession…**because the Lord loved you.**"*
(DEUTERONOMY 7:6 & 8)

From the first pages of Genesis, we see the holy, just and righteous God wanting fellowship with human beings. In fact, He created them for that purpose. He delighted in their company in the cool of the day. Then, by preferring their own way to His, they lost that close companionship.

There were exceptions. Genesis chapters 5 & 6 record that Enoch and Noah walked with God. But after the flood and before Noah's death, mankind had already returned to violent, evil ways.

Then the Lord set His focus on Abraham, Isaac and Jacob as well as on the nation that grew out of this family. We watch this love story unfold throughout the rest of the Old Testament. In the passage above from Deuteronomy, the Lord was assuring the people of Israel of His *"unfailing love"* for them. He spoke to Israel at times as a father but even more often as a lover and husband longing for them to return the love He felt for them.

When God found a tender heart like David's, He expressed with immense delight, *"I have found David…a man after my own heart."* (Acts 13:22) He even exclaimed to Israel, *"I will sing for the one I love."* (Isaiah 5:1)

When the Queen of Sheba visited Solomon, God's love for His people was so evident to her, she asserted, *"Because of the Lord's eternal love for Israel…"* (1 Kings 10:9)

Even when Israel turned away from the Lord, His love for her remained. Hear His tender, deep lament in Hosea 11:8, *"How can I give you up…?"*

The heavenly Father calls His Hebrew people, *"My beloved,"* (Jeremiah 11:15) and *"the one I love."* (Jeremiah 12:7) He declares, *"You are precious… in my sight…I love you,"* (Isaiah 43:4) *"my unfailing love for you will not be shaken."* (Isaiah 54:10)

The love of the **Lord Jesus** for **His people, Israel,** is never more poignant than on the day of His triumphal entry into Jerusalem. *"As he approached… the city, **he wept over it** and said, 'If you, even you, had only known on this day what would bring you peace.'"* (Luke 19:41 & 42)

Even though the apostle Paul was sent to the Gentiles, the Lord gave him such a love for *"**his brothers…the people of Israel**"* that he states he could wish himself **cut off from the Lord** if it would mean that they would come to Him. (Romans 9:3)

Lord, we thank You for such extraordinary and eternal love for this people, Israel. We do not understand all the reasons why You chose to set Your love on a particular people, but we trust You, our just, wise and faithful God. Your plan is perfect! You will reveal to us what You want us to know.

PERSONAL REFLECTION

I am His "treasured possession". The Lord my God has chosen me, because the Lord loved me. (I am a Gentile) When the tears flow yet again, it is because I find it difficult to take in, the full truth, that GOD loves me as I am, warts and all. I am HIS and HE is mine, forever.

A Forever Covenant

*"I will establish my covenant as an **everlasting covenant** between me and you and your descendants after you for the generations to come."* (GENESIS 17:7)

In ancient times, a covenant was the most binding contract one could make with another – far more serious than anything we can understand today. Modern society has nothing that comes close to its equivalent. The possibility of breaking covenant was unthinkable.

In the passage above, **Almighty God Himself** was making a covenant with Abraham that was to **last forever**. He renewed that everlasting covenant with Isaac, (Genesis 26:3 & 4) and then with Jacob. (Genesis 28:13-15) **By the Lord's sovereign choice, He was setting His attention on a man, Abraham, and specific descendants of his, Isaac and Jacob, and their posterity.**

In this age of egalitarianism, the Lord's Sovereign choice is a difficult concept. Perhaps it helps to look at this choice as a difference in function. God was calling Israel – the name first given to Jacob and by extension, to his descendants – to a specific purpose in history. In the midst of a totally pagan world that had no remembrance of the one, true God, He injected Himself into the life of a man and his family to make a covenant with them that was designed to go on forever, in order to accomplish His will on the earth.

The word "forever" is used numerous times throughout Genesis and other Scriptures regarding this covenant. In spite of Israel's rebellion, the Lord declared in Judges 2:1, *"I will **never** break my covenant with you."*

In Psalm 89:34 the Lord vowed: *"I will not violate my covenant or alter what my lips have uttered."*

King David reminded his nation the day he brought the Ark of the Covenant back to Jerusalem: *"He (the Lord) remembers **his covenant forever**, the word he commanded to a thousand generations."* (Psalms 105:8 & I Chronicles 16:15)

In light of these declarations by the Lord God, can we doubt that He will keep His covenant with His ancient people? *"God is not a man, that he should lie."* (Numbers 23:19) **If the Lord does not keep Covenant with Israel, what assurance do we Christians have that He will be faithful to us, the Church?**

———

Lord, we're at Day 2 in this study, and we're already being stretched as we try to grasp these challenging concepts. We acknowledge that we need Your help. Speak to our hearts so that we can understand this special covenant relationship You have with Your ancient people, Israel.

May we know that Your keeping covenant with them is visible proof that You will also keep covenant with the Church You bought with Your own blood.

PERSONAL REFLECTION

God is faithfull. He will keep Covenant with Israel.
So we are assured that God will be faithful to us,
His Church.
I do acknowledge that we need your help. Speak
to my heart Lord so that I can understand the special
covenant relationship You have with Your ancient people,
Israel, and You will keep covenant with the Church, You
bought with Your own blood.

The Land Is Integral To The Covenant

*"The Lord said to Abram '...look north and south, east and west. All the **land** that you see I will give to you and your offspring **forever**.'"* (GENESIS 13:14 & 15)

Without smog, Abraham could see a very long way from the mountains of Israel! In the Genesis 17 passage we studied on Day 2, the Lord continues in v.8, **"The whole land of Canaan, where you are now an alien, I will give as an everlasting possession to you."**

This is confirmed to Jacob. **"I am God Almighty...The land I gave to Abraham and Isaac I also give to you, and...to your descendants."** (Genesis 35:12)

The book of Deuteronomy describes the Lord's comments and final instructions before Israel entered the land after their forty years of wandering in the desert. The Lord is very forthright: *"It is not because of your righteousness or your integrity that you are going in to take possession of their land;"* (Deuteronomy 9:5) In fact, He says in chapter 31:21, *"I know what they are disposed to do, even before I bring them into the land I promised them on oath."*

We know from history that Israel rebelled against God until finally He sent them into exile. The first exile was for seventy years to Babylon, and the second has lasted for almost 2,000 years – beginning 40 years after Jesus wept over them and warned them of what was coming.

But even before Israel entered the land the first time, Moses' words to them provide us with a glimpse of the Lord's future plan.

> *"When all these blessings and curses* (see Deuteronomy 28 & 29) *come upon you...wherever the Lord your God disperses you among the nations, and when you and your children return to the Lord...God will...have compassion on you and gather you again from all the nations. ...God... will bring you to the land that belonged to your fathers, and you will take possession of it."* (Deuteronomy 30:1-5)

This covenant is not void! It is indeed forever! And it includes the land, a portion of which we again see in Israel's possession today.

Have all those Israelis who are now back in the land *"returned to the Lord"?* (Deuteronomy 30:2) No. But many have. Others are coming to Him as they settle in their ancient towns and cities. Congregations are springing up everywhere, and Israeli friends tell us that there are now more followers of Yeshua (Jesus) in the land than there have been since the first century A.D.

There are also many godly Orthodox Jews who trust in the God of Abraham, Isaac and Jacob with all their hearts, who are waiting for Messiah to be revealed.

Lord, we join the many Jewish people in the land who are praying these words of David: *"Oh, that salvation for Israel would come out of Zion! When God restores the fortunes of his people, let Jacob rejoice and Israel be glad!"* (Psalm 53:6)

PERSONAL REFLECTION

I have returned to ELIM Pentecostal CHURCH after 25 (almost) years in a Baptist Church where the Lord God has set me free from a rebellious spirit. GOD, by HIS GRACE has also restored to me what "the locusts have eaten." I know that HIS hand is upon my life. I love the Lord Jesus deep down in my heart. I know he loves me and I am known inside and out. I am fully accepted by the True and living God in Jesus Christ. All praise to the God of Zion in Israel.

Engraved On The Palms Of His Hands

"For the Lord comforts his people

and will have compassion on his afflicted ones.

But Zion said, 'the Lord has forsaken me…'

Can a mother forget the baby at her breast

and have no compassion on the child she has borne?

Though she may forget,

I will not forget you!

See, I have engraved you on the palms of my hands."

(ISAIAH 49:13-16)

I remember a tense moment in a gathering of Christians and Jews just before the movie, "The Passion of the Christ," was released. The question was asked, "Did the Jews put Jesus on the cross?" Every eye was riveted on the speaker. "No!" he said. "Our sins put Jesus on the cross!" Oh! If only the Church had given such an answer down through its history!

So many Christians through the centuries have believed not only that the Jews were responsible for Jesus' death but also that God has utterly forsaken them. These Christians think the Church has completely taken the place of the Jewish people as the "Chosen" of God. The history of most of the last 2,000 years would seem to support their belief.

However, we have examined the Lord's promises that **His love** and **His Covenant** are forever. Does "forever" not apply as well to the last two millennia? Perhaps the following Scriptures give us a clue.

"For a brief moment I abandoned you, (Remember 1,000 years is as a day)

but with deep compassion I will bring you back.

…I hid my face from you for a moment,

*But with **everlasting** kindness I will have compassion on you."* (Isaiah 54: 7 & 8)

"No longer will they call you Deserted, or name your land Desolate.
…for the Lord will take delight in you." (Isaiah 62:4)

"I will plant her for myself in the land;
I will show my love to the one I called 'Not my loved one.'
I will say to those called 'Not my people,'
'You are my people';
and they will say, 'You are my God.'" (Hosea 2:23)

Paul asks the believers in Rome who were struggling with anti-Jewish emotions: *"Did God reject his people? … Did they stumble so as to fall **beyond recovery?"***

"Not at all!" comes his resounding answer. (Romans 11:1&11)

Lord, thank you that You have not forgotten or rejected Your ancient people. You are a faithful God who keeps Covenant and loves unconditionally. Thank You that You are again showing Your compassion to the Jewish people. Help us to love those whom You love – **those who are** *"engraved on the palms of (Your) hands."*

PERSONAL REFLECTION

I thank the Lord God for leading me in the paths of Righteousness, to know the TRUTH about God in Jesus. I too believe that I'm "engraved" on the palms of His hands. "By My wounds you are healed" said the Lord Jesus. I have claimed HIS healing power for others, and I also believe He was the perfect sacrifice needed to take our punishment on the cross. Praise the Lord.

A Look Into History

"…do not boast… Do not be arrogant."

(ROMANS 11:18 & 20)

A devotional may seem to be a strange place to discuss history. Sadly however, many in the Church today have no idea how much persecution has been inflicted on the Jewish people in the name of Christ. So our key Scripture for today is Paul's warning resounding down through the centuries to all who will hear: "Do not be arrogant." Regrettably, many have ignored Paul's plea.

The apostles were scarcely in their graves when key leaders in the early church began turning against the Jews. By the time Christianity became accepted throughout the Roman Empire, every vestige of Jewishness had been erased from the Church. Jewish people who became Christians were forbidden to keep Saturday as the Sabbath, or to celebrate the feasts commanded by the Lord through Moses.

Expulsion, forced conversion and violence mar the pages of the history of Christian Europe as the separation between Christian and Jew continued to widen. Even many of the holiest and most respected church fathers were virulently anti-Semitic. [1]

The Crusades, between 1000 and 1200 A.D., became an excuse to eradicate as many Jews as possible as fanatic knights and their followers rampaged through cities and towns on their way to the Holy Land. Once in Jerusalem, these men, convinced they were doing God's will, slaughtered Jews as well as Muslims until the blood literally ran through the streets.

In Europe in the late 1200s, a story circulated widely that Jews were kidnapping Christian children, slaughtering them, drinking their blood and using it to make their Passover bread. Untold thousands of Jewish people lost their lives in the ensuing centuries because of this preposterous lie. These accusations continued in Eastern Europe well into the last century and still surface today in Muslim countries. How difficult this is to comprehend!

Down through the centuries, persecutions and mass expulsions took place in England, France, Spain, Russia and Eastern Europe. Between 1440 and 1808, 30,000 Jews were burned at the stake in Spain and thousands more in Portugal and Mexico.

Even Martin Luther (1500s) in his later years joined the ranks of those who vilified the Jews and desired their destruction. It has been said that Luther's angry outbursts against the Jewish people helped Hitler justify his purges and death camps.

It is estimated that in the centuries **before** the Holocaust 7,000,000 Jewish people were slaughtered by those confessing to be Christians. Then during World War II another 6,000,000 were annihilated.

Where was the Lord in all those centuries of suffering? I believe He was weeping with His people. *"In all their affliction He was afflicted."* (Isaiah 63:9 NKJV) He was also weeping over His Church. He had left such clear instructions to love.

Lord, what horrors You have looked upon! Our hearts break that Paul's warning was not heeded and that the Jewish people have had to suffer so intensely for so long! Cleanse us, Your Church, from any remaining arrogance.

PERSONAL REFLECTION

Even today in October 2014 There is still a strong spirit of arrogants in the Church. I only very recently was a victim of it and I left the church and am now in an ELIM pentecostal Church where I have found a freedom to be used in the gifts of the Holy Spirit. I love them all/especially -the people, when we are singing the songs or choruses together in harmony, Praiseing our Lord God together in 'love' with everyone. P.T.L. Amen.

19

Christians Who Cared

"Comfort, comfort my people, says your God."

(ISAIAH 40:1)

D r. Michael Brown has written a powerful book entitled *Our Hands Are Stained with Blood – The Tragic Story of the "Church" and the Jewish People*. In the midst of recounting the horrific mistreatment of Jews, Dr. Brown gives us a wonderful chapter entitled, "A Blessed and Beautiful Stream," in which he acquaints the reader with a few of those who have stood out in history against this tide of anti-Semitic evil.

Of course many of these believers were the quiet ones who remained in obscurity. They were those who cried out to God in prayer for the Jewish people or who performed secret acts of kindness despite the personal danger. We know that many of these "righteous Gentiles," (as the Jewish people call Christians who care for them) gave their lives to save Jews during the Holocaust. Corrie ten Boom's family is one of the best-known examples (as depicted in the book and movie, *The Hiding Place*).

Interestingly, many of the Puritans who shaped early America had a vision for Israel and held the hope that the Jewish people would return to their land and their Lord. Perhaps one of the reasons God has so blessed America has been the fact that many times through the years we have opened our arms to Jewish people fleeing the persecutions of Europe.

Samuel Rutherford, a famous Scottish Puritan, had a deep love for the Lord and His ancient people. I love this description from one of his letters quoted in Dr. Brown's book:

> O to see the sight, next to Christ's Coming in the clouds, the most joyful! Our elder brother the Jews and Christ fall upon one another's neck... They have been long asunder; ... O longed-for and lovely day-dawn! ...let me see that sight which will be as life from the dead, Thee and Thy ancient people in mutual embraces.[2]

In the early 1800s, the London Jews Society was formed. This organization encouraged Jews to immigrate to Israel and also established the first Protestant Jewish Church there. They opened schools and a hospital. The result was that, for the first time in 1,700 years, there were known to be Jewish people in Israel who came to believe in Jesus as the Messiah. During the intense persecutions in Russia in the 1880s, the London Jews Society helped the first Russian immigrants "home" to Israel.

Even Queen Victoria, who reigned on the British throne for more than 50 years in the last half of the 1800s, strongly supported a homeland for the Jewish people.

In today's Scripture from Isaiah, whom is the Lord addressing? Could it be that He is actually stirring all of us in the Church to *"comfort"* **His** chosen people? I believe so!

Thank You, Lord, that You have always had a faithful remnant in the Church who has understood Your great heart of love for Your covenant people. Thank You that down through the centuries there have been those who have heeded Paul's warnings and have blessed the Jews. May there be more and more Christians who are inspired to *"comfort"* with an unconditional love, these dear people who have suffered so much.

PERSONAL REFLECTION

I am now in a group of mixed race and led by a couple who lead the prayer group and are Jewish. We pray for ISRAEL. The enemy is back in many ways. We have to remember, Jesus WON THE VICTORY, over death, and now we need to keep close to the Lord God, for His Guidance, every day. I pray openly in the group and the people have accepted my presence among them. Thanks be to God our Father.

World War II And The Holocaust

"You who call on the Lord, give yourselves no rest,
and give him no rest (pray continually) till he establishes
Jerusalem and makes her the praise of the earth."

(ISAIAH 62:6 & 7)

In the summer of 2004, as I walked for the first time through Yad Vashem, the Holocaust Memorial in Jerusalem, what struck me most deeply was the Jewish suffering **after** World War II. My heart was broken not only by the gas chambers and crematoriums (which I had known about) but also by the post-war holding camps in Cyprus and northern Europe, where conditions were not much better than at Auschwitz. I wept as I thought of the survivors of the Holocaust finally landing in Haifa, Israel, only to be sent back to the holding camps because of anti-Semitic regulations.

But I don't intend here to dwell on the horrors. If you have seen "Schindler's List," "Playing for Time" or "The Pianist," you know very well the appalling scenes from the Warsaw ghetto and the death camps.

Instead, let us zero in on a small Bible College in Wales where nightly, powerful prayer meetings were occurring during the war. Rees Howells, an intercessor God had groomed with great care, would take time by himself to wait on the Lord for the prayer strategy for a particular evening.

Once he had heard the Lord's direction, he would join others already in prayer and together they would go into deep intercession – perhaps for hours – until they sensed they had "broken through" and the Lord had achieved what He desired. Often within days the news would report a victory the Allies had needed to press on to defeat the evil Nazi regime – exactly as they had prayed.

O yes, there were prayer gatherings everywhere as the world writhed convulsively during those awful years between 1939-1945. Finally those regimes fell, and the senseless murder ceased for those whose only crime was that they were Jewish.

Can we ever answer the question "Why?" In today's world, innocent people, children, and babies are being murdered almost daily by terrorists. We all wrestle with why evil has to be so powerful. The answers will come when we see the Lord face to face.

Then, we will have the kind of history lesson those two disciples had on the road to Emmaus on Resurrection Day, when the Lord Jesus brought His gruesome death and the prophetic Word together for them. (Luke 24) Until that day, I have to trust my Lord. In His Sovereignty, the Lord had to allow the Holocaust. The outcome was a homeland for the Jewish people – the restored nation of Israel. He used the incredible tragedy for His purposes.

To return to our opening Scripture, we see that intercessors **did** call on the Lord and gave themselves and Him no rest during those terrible years. Through the horrors, the Lord somehow caused His Will to be done to bring closer the Day He *"establishes Jerusalem and makes her the praise of the earth."*

Father, again we have to acknowledge that Your ways are not our ways. (Isaiah 55:8) We can only declare that You are Sovereign over all the earth. You know what You are doing as You bring about Your will and Your purposes in preparation for that great Day!

PERSONAL REFLECTION

As I was an evacuee of 6–10 years of age, I only read on the T.V. as films were shown about the war years. I wasn't old enough to know any jewish people. Now, the Lord God has led me to be in prayer groups to join them into prayer for Israel, and another group that pray for the alior routes to be kept open and make ready for the Chosen People of God to return to Israel, also to pray for their protection as the enemy is attacking Israel again.

The Time To Favor Zion

"But You, O Lord, sit enthroned forever;
...You will arise and have compassion on Zion,
for it is time to show favor to her;
the appointed time has come." (PSALM 102:12 & 13)

DAY 8

I will never forget the gathering in the large cafeteria of a major industrial company in Cleveland, Ohio. Derek Prince was addressing two thousand eager listeners. The year was 1971 – twenty-three years after the formation of the state of Israel. The air was electric as we heard this renowned Bible teacher expound on how this verse related to Israel's birth as a nation.

Profound questions were being addressed: Had 1948 been a turning point in history? One of the Lord's "suddenlies"? An appointed time that had escaped the world's attention, but to the Lord was of great importance? Was He showing favor to His people, Israel, today in the midst of our modern world?

We knew the new nation had been created, but here was Scriptural insight into what the Lord thought of the event. I was in awe as my mind flashed back to mother's words: "Maybe that's what the prophets meant!"

The following two Scriptures give us further insights into this *"appointed time."* Jesus, in His prophetic description of the history we have just studied, tells us: *"Jerusalem will be trampled on by the Gentiles **until** the times of the Gentiles are fulfilled."* (Luke 21:24) Paul echoes this: *"Israel has experienced a hardening in part **until** the full number of the Gentiles has come in."* (Romans 11:25)

With Israel's birth, a seismic shift occurred in the heavenly realm and in the world. And many – even much of the Church with its rich depository of Scriptural truth – missed it. How comparable to the way the world missed our Savior's birth, which was ushered in by the great angelic pronouncement. The sky was ablaze with heavenly light for the Bethlehem shepherds. And the sleeping world yawned.

So it was also with Israel's inception as a nation. Few understood or were even aware of God's dramatic invasion into history. But the process had begun. For indeed, the *"Lord hears the needy and does not despise his captive people. ...for God will save Zion and rebuild the cities of Judah."* (Psalm 69:33 & 35) And that is exactly what has been happening since 1948.

Father, please help us all in Your Church to see the significance of the wondrous accomplishment that You brought forth from the ashes of the Holocaust. You were true to Your Covenant and again gave Your people their land. You have had *"compassion on Zion"* and shown her favor at *"the appointed time,"* just as You promised! You are revealing the continuation of Your love story.

PERSONAL REFLECTION

When ever God does something His way, there is NO FEAR. He moves people into crying tears with compassion for I half have escperianced it and know that the Holy Spirit of God is also weeping with the compassion of God in me. I have wept recently for about 20 minutes or more knowing that while I was crying I didn't know why I was crying, but I conected the tears were for the Jewish people as the only reason that made sense to me. P.T.L.

Can A Nation Be Born In A Day?

"Who has ever heard of such a thing?
…Can a country be born in a day
or a nation be brought forth in a moment?
Yet no sooner is Zion in labor
than she gives birth to her children.
Do I bring to the moment of birth
and not give delivery?" says the Lord. (ISAIAH 66: 8 & 9)

Let's return briefly to the Bible College in Wales. In 1947, a number of the young students there sensed the Lord asking them to temporarily lay down their missionary calls and stay to intercede for the birth of the State of Israel. "We pleaded," wrote Rees Howells in his diary, "that because of His **covenant** with Abraham 4,000 years ago, God would take His people back to their land, and Palestine [3] should again become a Jewish State." [4]

On the day of the mandatory United Nations' vote to allow Israel's status as a sovereign nation, there was much prayer. The first vote did not pass. The college intercessors went back into more intense prayer and believed they saw "God's angels influencing those men in the United Nations Conference to work on behalf of God's people." The next day the news came of the needed two-thirds majority. The college proclaimed November 28, 1947, "one of the greatest days for the Holy Spirit in the history of these 2,000 years." [5]

Fighting continued for the next five months between the Arab nations and the Jewish people. However in May 1948, the Jewish council in Jerusalem signed Israel's Declaration of Independence. Modern Israel was *"born in a day."*

In less than 24 hours, seven Arab countries declared war against this new state.

Miraculously this fledgling, ill-equipped nation was victorious. Even after she was attacked again in 1967, her forces prevailed and broke through to the Western Wall – all that was left of the Old Temple. At that moment all of Jerusalem came back into Jewish hands for the first time since they were exiled to Babylon 600 years before Christ. [6]

Another attack against Israel occurred in 1973 on Yom Kippur, the Day of Atonement. Syria and Egypt chose the holiest day in the Jewish calendar when almost everyone in Israel fasts, for a massive attack. Israeli soldiers rushed to the Golan and fought for several days without a meal. For some unknown reason, Syrian tanks suddenly stopped dead in their tracks, and her army became confused. There were also reports of people seeing a large Hand in the sky over the Golan Heights, east of the Sea of Galilee. Many Israelis believe that God directly intervened and helped them survive the worst of their wars.

God is again protecting His people as He reestablishes them in their land. *"'He who scattered Israel* **will gather** *them and* **will watch over** *his flock like a shepherd.' For the Lord will ransom Jacob and redeem them from the hand of those stronger than they."* (Jeremiah 31:10 & 11)

Faithful God, thank You that You did *"bring to the moment of birth"* and You did give delivery. Thank You that You have protected Israel in the ensuing wars. We will *"Rejoice with Jerusalem and be glad for her."* (Isaiah 66:10)

PERSONAL REFLECTION

God is faithful, and I too thank You Father God for the many times you have helped me in my life. I thank You Father for your love for us all who are yours. I pray that the two different prayer groups that I go to will hear from God and the Holy Spirit reveal words and use us in the gifts as we pray for Israel and Jerusalem. That many more Jews will return home.

They Will Rebuild

"I will bring back my exiled people Israel;
they will rebuild *the ruined cities and live in them.*
They will plant vineyards and drink their wine;
they will make gardens and eat their fruit.
I will plant Israel in their own land,
never again to be uprooted from the land I have given them,"
says the Lord your God. (AMOS 9:14 & 15)

The transformation of the land of Israel from mosquito-infested swamps and barren desert to productive farms, vineyards and orchards is amazing. The Lord has blessed Israelis' hard work. One indication is the jet stream, which actually shifted so that some of the former desert land has regular rain again.

Millions of trees have been planted on the barren slopes – many by Christians. Each visit my husband and I make to Israel we see Isaiah 51:3 becoming more of a reality. The Lord *"will make her deserts like Eden, her wastelands like the garden of the Lord."*

For many years now, Israeli jets have departed nightly full of fruit and flowers for the tables of Europe – a direct fulfillment of Isaiah 27:6, *"In days to come Jacob will take root, Israel will bud and blossom and fill all the world with fruit."* Even in the grocery stores of America we can now purchase Israeli fresh produce.

In the Negev desert, exceptional olive orchards and vineyards are developing using brackish water pumped from thousands of feet below ground.

"They…will renew the ruined cities that have been devastated for generations." (Isaiah 61:4) The rebuilding has been intense throughout the years of Israel's existence. Their ability to absorb and house new immigrants is astounding. Their rebuilt cities are clean and orderly.

Never before in history has a dead language been revived. Yet in Israel today, Hebrew is spoken everywhere and immigrants are required to attend Hebrew classes upon arrival.

Never before has a nation, which was dispersed into many countries, remained intact as a distinct people. Ethnic groups have always been absorbed after a few generations. Yet the Lord has kept Israel as a nation even in her long exile.

The Lord has remembered **His covenant** and **His everlasting love** for His nation. The time to favor Zion has come.

Gracious Father, You have looked down on this people throughout the generations and yearned for this time when You could again pour out Your blessings upon them. Thank You for all that is being fulfilled and all that will yet happen in order to complete Your great plan of Redemption for Israel and all peoples.

PERSONAL REFLECTION

As a member of C.C. and J. (Council of Christians and Jews, I am involved in praying for Jewish people to return to Israel. Having gone to Israel, and stayed about 8 days, I had the experience of helping a Jewish man called Jacob, in the time of asking him to be Healed of a throat cancer. He was violently prayed for, for the cancer to leave him. etc; I don't know if God answered the prayer. God was in that place. becaus it was recorded not only many miracles P.T.L. happened but many gave their lives to Jesus and was Saved. P.T.L

The Lord's Purposes On The Earth

"For Adonai (the Lord) will fulfill his word on the earth with certainty and without delay."

DAY 11

(ROMANS 9:28, COMPLETE JEWISH BIBLE)

After studying the history of the Jewish people and before we move on to more recent events, let us step back to look at the big picture of the Lord's priorities. How is He fulfilling His Word *"on the earth with certainty and without delay"*?

First, the Gospel is spreading across the face of the earth at a staggering pace. Bible translators are now using advanced computer technology to speed their vital work. The Internet is making the Gospel available to millions previously without access to its message. Thousands are daily risking their lives to obey the Lord's command to *"go and make disciples of all nations."* (Matthew 28:19)

Also in His discourse with His disciples concerning the time of His return, the Lord Jesus gave these same marching orders: *"And this Gospel of the Kingdom will be preached in the whole world as a testimony to all nations, and then the end shall come."* (Matthew 24:14)

We read John's vision in Revelation 7:9 of the *"great multitude that no one could count, from every nation, tribe, people and language, standing before the throne and in front of the Lamb."* And we are stirred to pray harder, give more and go where the Lord sends us that the maximum number of people may come into His Kingdom.

Another of the Lord's priorities is His Church, whom He loves so passionately that He calls her His Bride. Much of the emphasis in the letters of Paul, Peter and John is on teaching the followers of Jesus how to grow up in Him, turn from worldly ways, walk with Him and love others as He did. We are to be *"without stain or wrinkle or any other blemish, but holy and blameless."* (Ephesians 5:27)

The Lord Jesus is at the right hand of the Father interceding for us that we, His Bride, will make ourselves ready for His coming. (Revelation 19:7) He will help us but **we** must prepare. We must continually walk more closely with Him, our beloved Bridegroom.

Almost obscured from the Church's view is a third priority – a distinct stream flowing through the Scriptures – the return of the Jews to their land and their restoration to their Lord. This stream is an integral part of the river of God's great purposes on the earth. For most of the past 2,000 years this priority has been flowing underground. But this stream is bursting forth as a powerful reality in our day to take its rightful place in the Church.

My desire in this devotional is to set before you just a portion of the tremendous weight of evidence in the Scriptures that the physical and spiritual restoration of Israel is absolutely essential in the Lord's big picture. His Word cannot be fulfilled on the earth without the promises in the Old Testament Prophets concerning Israel coming to pass.

Father of Love, please keep revealing to us Your heart in this matter. We know You will have to open our eyes so we can see how Israel fits into Your amazing plans for the end of the age and Your return.

PERSONAL REFLECTION

God chose Israel, among all the other nations. They are now knowing that Jesus is the Massiah, and born a Jew. They now beleive it. There are thousands arriving back into the Israely airport. I, with many others mainly Gentiles, preparing the Aliah ways open. We are praying for the stones to be removed. We are involved by reading aloud proclamations of repentance of the past, by the way we did not help the Jews as we aught to have. Only God knows if we have done enough. There is more to do yet.

31

Aliyah

"This is what Cyrus king of Persia says: '...Anyone of His people among you – may the Lord his God be with him and let him go up.'" (II CHRONICLES 36:23)

"Aliyah" is a Hebrew word that literally means "to go up" or "ascend." In the passage above, King Cyrus was giving his blessing to Jewish people who wished to return or *"go up"* to rebuild Jerusalem and other areas of Israel after their 70 years of captivity in Babylon.

There are approximately 70 passages in the Bible that refer to the return of the Jewish people to their land. Some verses specify that it will be *"in the latter days."* Other Scriptures speak of this migration coming from every corner of the earth. In many places the Lord declares explicitly and emphatically, *"I will bring you back."*

When Israel became a nation in 1948 and the restrictions on immigration were finally lifted, Jews who had survived the ravages of the Holocaust poured into their "Promised Land" from countries across Europe.

In addition, they fled from all the surrounding Arab countries, including 47,000 Jews from Yemen. From Morocco 170,000 returned, and 14,000 came from Algeria. There were 104,000 Jews who literally had to be smuggled "home" out of Iraq. Between 1948 and 1955, the Jewish population in Israel doubled.

Almost 30,000 have been rescued from tyrannical regimes in Ethiopia. In one weekend in the early 1990s, 14,400 were taken home on Israeli El-Al commercial airliners just 36 hours before the Ethiopian airport was attacked and closed by advancing Marxist rebels. At one point there were 24 jumbo jets without seats (to carry maximum capacity) ferrying back and forth from Ethiopia to Israel to complete the rescue.

Surely this was one of the fulfillments of Isaiah 60:8. *"Who are these that fly along like clouds, like doves to their nests?"* What an accurate description of a return home by airplane – 2,600 years before the advent of air travel!

Israel has welcomed her people home from every corner of the earth since 1948. Their assimilation into Israeli society has been remarkable considering all the cultural and language differences that challenge the new arrivals.

The Lord is working out His promises to Jewish people before our very eyes. And we have yet to see the greatest and most glorious aspects of what He will do. Jeremiah describes an aliyah yet to come that will overshadow the great Exodus out of Egypt.

> *"However, the days are coming," declares the Lord, "when men will no longer say 'As surely as the Lord lives, who brought the Israelites out of Egypt,' but they will say, 'As surely as the Lord lives, who brought the Israelites up out of the land of the north and out of **all the countries** where he had banished them.' **For I will restore them to the land I gave their forefathers."** (Jeremiah 16:14 & 15)*

Thank You, Lord God of Abraham, Isaac and Jacob, for fulfilling Your promises to Israel's forefathers that their descendants would return to the land You gave them. We believe that You will never forget what You have spoken until all is fulfilled. We give You glory for Your faithfulness!

PERSONAL REFLECTION

This is the year, 2014 october 16ᵗʰ as I write. We the group of c,c. and J. are about to complete the aliah/highway from Scotland down through to London. In London we are about to read some more proclamations to do with "the Golden Curtain". ie: The Bank of England, has the gold which in the past was taken from Scotland and claimed the ground and much more from them, killing and taking over all their goods and land.

Prepare The Way

"Build up, build up, prepare the road!
Remove the obstacles out of the way of my people."

(ISAIAH 57:14)

DAY 13

The focus of our study on Day 12 was how the Lord worked miracles to fulfill His word and bring home thousands from Europe and the countries surrounding Israel. What about the more than 2,000,000 Jewish people who were virtual prisoners of the communist system in all the countries of the Soviet Empire? A small number were allowed to emigrate each year, but many were being watched and imprisoned without cause.

In 1985, a group of international prayer leaders gathered in Jerusalem for a major prayer conference that was convened to intercede specifically for the release of the Soviet Jews. The Lord had been preparing the hearts of some of the men, and during the gathering, they agreed to take a prayer journey behind the Iron Curtain.

What followed was amazing. Skirting the Russian KGB, these intercessors prayed powerful prayers for the release of Soviet Jews in front of the Kremlin, the statues of Lenin and even the headquarters of the KGB itself.

They traveled to Odessa in the Ukraine, to the famous Potemkin Steps, which lead from the port up an embankment into the city. Invaders through the centuries scaled those steps as their point of entry. The most recent had been the Nazis bent on conquering the Ukraine and destroying the large Jewish population of the country. The intercessors descended the long stairway – praying again for the Jews' release as they went. As they turned at the bottom to ascend the stairs, they almost bumped into the KGB agents who were following closely behind them, trying to figure out what these odd tourists were doing.

Suddenly, cracks in the Iron Curtain began to appear. In front of the Berlin Wall in June 1987, President Reagan announced, "This wall will fall." And yes, down it came and ruthless regimes toppled. The peoples held captive by communism had their first taste of freedom! The Lord had heard the prayers of those intercessors as well as the worldwide prayer that had ascended to His throne during the 70 years of Soviet domination.

As a result, in 1990 alone, more than 185,000 Jewish people left the former Soviet Union for Israel. In 2002 that number reached 1,000,000 immigrants (in 12 years), helping to fulfill Isaiah 49:25 (NKJV)

"Even the captives of the mighty shall be taken away, And the prey of the terrible be delivered." (How terrible the communist massacres were.)

Look at how specifically the Scriptures apply to the aliyah (return) from Russia, the land whose capital, Moscow, is directly north of Israel.

"I (the Lord) will say to the north, 'Give them up!'" (Isaiah 43:6)

"See, I will bring them from the land of the north." (Jeremiah 31:8)

"'Come! Come! Flee from the land of the north,' declares the Lord." (Zechariah 2:6)

So yes, *"the obstacles"* are being removed and there is a highway for *"my people"* to go home from *"the land of the north."*

Lord, what a privilege to be alive in a day when Your Word is being fulfilled before our eyes. Thank You for all those who have been faithful to pray! May Your Jewish people still in the *"land of the north"* return to their homeland!

PERSONAL REFLECTION

I am in a prayergroup that meets once a month and we are gathered to hear the updates of the work that God is doing in Israel. Many groups and families are flying "like doves" to their home in Israel, Jerusalem. I have joined them and God Willing, I will be there next meeting. It is a privilege to be involved in such a time as seeing the Chosen people being flown out back to Israel.

God Has Called The Gentiles To Help

DAY 14

"This is what the Sovereign Lord says:
'See I will beckon to the Gentiles,
*...they will bring your sons in their arms
and carry your daughters on their shoulders.'"*

(ISAIAH 49:22)

As the doors of the former Soviet Union opened in the early 1990s, those who had made the prayer journeys and other Christian leaders recognized that the above Scripture was a mandate to **Gentile** believers to be involved in assisting the Soviet Jews "home." A number of Christian groups began making help available across the former Soviet Union.

Gustav Scheller, the founder of Operation Exodus, (Ebenezer Emergency Fund) believed God was calling him to use a ship as well as airplanes to help Jewish people "home." After much prayer and intensive negotiation with the Ukrainian and Israeli governments, a shipping route opened. In 1991, a ship began carrying Jewish families and Holocaust survivors from the port of Odessa in the Ukraine, across the Black Sea, through the Bosporus, under the bridges of Istanbul, and past the Greek islands into the Mediterranean Sea to Haifa, Israel.

Isaiah 60:9 speaks of *"the ships of Tarshish* (or trading ships), *bringing your sons from afar, with their silver and their gold, to the honor of the Lord your God, the Holy One of Israel."*

I remember the time in 1996 when my husband, our daughter and I had the privilege of accompanying these dear Jewish people as they made aliyah on the ship. When they first arrived at the base camp in Odessa, some of them mistrusted those of us who were trying to help. (I don't blame them – after all that their parents and ancestors had endured at the hands of Christians.) But after a few days at sea together, we couldn't stroll the decks without being hugged and thanked for helping them to immigrate to Israel. Many of these Jews had the sense they were being drawn home. Some of them stated that it was definitely the God of Israel who was compelling them to return.

There were 172 sailings between 1991 and 2004. The Lord protected those journeys from stormy seas, from intransigent bureaucrats, from unlit fishing boats directly in the ship's path and from many other dangers.

When helping Jewish people return by air, Operation Exodus and other groups work together with the Jewish Agency. This Israeli based organization, established to assist immigration, charters airline flights from the major cities across western Russia, Siberia and the Russian Far East. Western volunteers work closely with Russian Christians to help Jewish people find documents that prove they are Jewish. Often any trace of their Jewishness has been destroyed during the years of persecution. But the Lord is working miracles to help them find their documents in far-away archives, receive visas from Israeli consuls, and be transported by the volunteers long distances to the nearest airport.

Whether returning by ship or air, at the moment of landing in Israel, the new arrivals experience such a sense of joy and completeness. They know they are finally "home."

Lord, we're so glad that You are having *"compassion on Jacob; once again* (You are choosing Israel and settling) *them in their own land."* (Isaiah 14:1) How wonderful that Gentile believers from so many nations are supporting them and escorting them home!

PERSONAL REFLECTION

From The Ends Of The Earth I Called You

DAY 15

"In that day the Lord will reach out his hand a second time to reclaim the remnant that is left of his people...

He ... will assemble the scattered people of Judah ***from the four quarters of the earth.***"

(ISAIAH 11:11 & 12)

There are few places on Earth much farther from Jerusalem than Siberia and the Far East of Russia. It was to those isolated places that the Communist dictators sent the political prisoners – many of whom were Jewish. Tens of thousands died as they built railroads and highways and worked in mines. On the Russian Chinese border is a city called Birobidzhan, which Stalin cruelly named the "New Jerusalem" for the Jews.

In a town many time zones east of Moscow, Ian, a volunteer in his late sixties from New Zealand, plodded through deep snow and biting cold to visit the Jewish people. His mission was to share Scriptures with them to show them that the time had come to "go home."

As hundreds of volunteers, young and old, from many nations have served throughout the former Soviet Union, they have witnessed amazing changes in the attitudes of the Jewish people. Many are unreceptive at first, but often as the volunteers read Scriptures to them from their ancient prophets, God's Word melts their hearts, and they decide to make preparation for their long journey to their new home.

Tears of joy welled up in my eyes in May 2004, as I stood in the Operation Exodus head office for the Far East of Russia. There before me was a large wall covered with photos of all the families, the young and the old, who had made aliyah in the last 12 years. What a moving sight – those dear faces!

These remote regions have also been the focus for aliyah-related work for the International Christian Embassy, Jerusalem. One of the areas where they work is above the Arctic Circle, where mines established during the Stalin era are now being closed and towns depopulated.

From there, Christian volunteers help Jewish people on a route that takes them through Finland to Israel.

I have heard numerous stories from these remote regions of the Lord's supernatural help for the valiant volunteers out in the Siberian winter. In one case, two of these young people drove to the top of a mountain pass only to find the road completely blocked with mounds of drifting snow. At that very moment, on that deserted road, two large trucks passed and blasted through the snow piles. The volunteers were then able to continue to another isolated village to search for and help more Jewish people.

> *"But you, O Israel, my servant,*
> *Jacob whom I have chosen,*
> *You descendants of Abraham, my friend,*
> *I took you from **the ends of the earth,***
> ***from its farthest corners I called you.***
> *...I have chosen you and not rejected you.*
> *So do not fear, for I am with you;*
> *do not be dismayed, for I am your God."* (Isaiah 41:8-10)

Yes, Lord, thank You that no place on Earth is too remote for You to find Your people. You scattered them, but now You are bringing them "home." Please continue to guide your servants to them. Please raise up many more intercessors to pray for this great work!

PERSONAL REFLECTION

With All My Heart And Soul

*"I will **surely** gather them from all the lands
where I banish them
...and will **assuredly** plant them in this land
with all my heart and soul."* (JEREMIAH 32:37 & 41)

DAY 16

If we take a moment to consider the Lord's incredibly great **heart of Love**, is it any wonder that He is once again demonstrating this love toward His chosen people? Or even that He would press into service Gentile believers, whose ancestors could well have been among those who persecuted so mercilessly down the centuries? Would He not invite His Gentile Church to *"speak tenderly to Jerusalem"* ? (Isaiah 40:2)

Throughout the former Soviet Union, we surely do see the Lord actively working, *"with all (His) heart and soul,"* to gather the Jewish people and plant them in their land. He is tenderly yet deliberately making a way where there seems to be none. Documents that were feared destroyed or lost, are amazingly found. Adamant customs officials unexpectedly relent, allowing families to emigrate. Homes in Israel become available for the aged. Families who had lost all hope that a brother or sister had survived, are reunited. Those who are sick, and even those given up for dead, are transported "home" to experience cutting-edge Israeli medical technology – and they recover.

The greatest demonstration of the Lord's intense engagement is the way He is touching Jewish hearts. Imagine the transformation, when Jewish people who once refused to listen to the Scriptures on aliyah, decide to sell their possessions and begin the process of immigration – taking all their worldly goods in a few suitcases. Only the Lord can convince these dear people to take such risks and start life all over again. It is nothing short of a miracle!

Let me tell you my favorite story involving the Lord's care on one of the voyages, as the ship carried His people home. During this particular sailing, the seas were exceptionally rough. Almost everyone was seasick. The Ebenezer staff and volunteers gathered to pray. On the second day, they became aware of the Lord's miraculous answer. The raging storm did not abate, but the ship seemed to be gliding smoothly in the midst of the high seas for the rest of the journey to the port of Haifa. The seasickness passed. The ship's crew was amazed. Everyone became intensely aware that the Lord was there in their midst – *"with all (His) heart and soul."*

What a fulfillment of Isaiah 43:16!

> *"This is what the Lord says –*
> *he who made a way through the sea,*
> **a path through the mighty waters."** *("raging waves"* – CJB)

Jeremiah 31:9 is equally relevant at this moment in history.

> *"They will come with weeping;*
> *they will pray as I bring them back.*
> *I will lead them…on a level path where they will not stumble,*
> **because I am Israel's father."**

We are indeed seeing the amazing beginning of that mighty work God said He will accomplish *"with all my heart and soul."*

O Lord, our hearts are so full of joy as we blend our voices with Isaiah 49:13:

> *"Shout for joy, O heavens;*
> *rejoice O earth;*
> *burst into song, O mountains!*
> *For the Lord comforts his people*
> *and will have compassion on his afflicted ones."* – *"with all (His) heart and soul!"*

PERSONAL REFLECTION

_____

_____

_____

_____

_____

_____

Not Leaving Any Behind

"Then they will know that I am the Lord their God, for
though I sent them into exile among the nations, I will
*gather them to their own land, **not leaving any behind.**"*
(EZEKIEL 39:28)

*"...and you, O Israelites, will be gathered up **one by one.**"*
(ISAIAH 27:12)

A young Jewish orphan was found homeless at a Ukrainian railway station. He was cared for until a family in Israel could be found to adopt him. Forty Israeli families responded to the newspaper ad, and soon he was on his way "home" – *"gathered up one by one."*

Just as in the first Exodus, the Lord is leading entire extended families out of captivity. In this case, the captivity isn't slavery. It's extreme poverty.

A single mother and her five children lived in such dire conditions in the Ukraine that the children routinely knocked on apartment doors to beg for food. The only pieces of furniture in their little, mud-floor apartment were two beds and a wardrobe. I never would have guessed the extent of their hardships when I met this smiling family on the ship bound for Israel. But this kind of destitution is common throughout the former Soviet Union.

There are instances where families with as many as 65 members immigrate together. Sometimes all the Jews from a synagogue will make aliyah. How that must please the heart of the Father!

Aliyah is beginning in other countries as well. In 2005, Israel opened its doors to a group from India – Jews who believe they belong to the ancient tribe of Manasseh. Later that same year, Jews living in transit camps in Ethiopia were again able to return at the rate of 600 a month – until all remaining 20,000 Ethiopian Jews are *"gathered"* home.

Studies since 1995 have shown that there are hundreds of thousands who may not even know they are Jewish in Latin America. Their identity has been hidden or lost because of persecution. They are beginning to learn of their Jewish roots. Some are preparing to make aliyah.

We do not know the Lord's timetable for gathering **all** the Jewish people back to the land. We do know that He will fulfill His Word exactly as He has promised.

In the 1700s, John Wesley wrote a hymn expressing the biblical truths we are studying in this devotional. One of the verses emphasizes Christians helping their Jewish brethren – *"not leaving any behind."*

> O that the chosen band
> Might now their brethren bring,
> And, gathered out of every land,
> Present to Zion's King!
> Of all the ancient race
> **Not one be left behind**
> But each, impelled by secret grace,
> His way to Canaan [7] find.

Yes, Lord, may none be left behind!

PERSONAL REFLECTION

A Banner For The Nations

"He will raise (or hoist) **a banner for the nations**
and gather the exiles of Israel;" (ISAIAH 11:12)

"I will set **a sign** *among them, (all nations and languages)*
...They will proclaim my glory among the nations.
And they will bring all your brothers (or kinsmen)
from all the nations, *to my holy mountain in Jerusalem*
as an offering to the Lord." (ISAIAH 66:19 & 20)

Down through history, a banner, an ensign or flag hoisted on a pole has been a means of making an important announcement. A king's ensign always flies over the place where he is in residence. The raising of a national flag announces victory for an army or a nation. The Lord expects the same kind of attention to be given when **He sets up a sign.**

"All you inhabitants of the world,
you who live on the earth:
when a banner is hoisted on the mountains, look!" (Isaiah 18:3 CJB)

In the first two verses cited above, aliyah is spoken of as a sign of great significance. So many times throughout the book of Ezekiel and the other Prophets, the Lord clearly announces the purpose of all He is doing in bringing His people back to the land. The *"banner"* is raised in order that Israel and *"the nations will know that I am the Lord."* (Ezekiel 36:23) This is His reason!

Here is an example of how this banner impacted one life. A Chinese intellectual actually came to faith in Jesus as he read the Old Testament Scriptures. He saw how accurately the biblical prophecies are being fulfilled in our day concerning the rebirth of Israel. He marveled that the preservation of the Jews as a distinct people is without precedent in history. Aliyah and the restoration of Israel are signs to those who will *"look."*

Thus we are indeed seeing the Lord draw attention to His purposes as He continues to show favor to Zion. The greatest aliyah is yet to come. It will be not only from areas where Jewish people are living in extreme hardship, not only from countries such as France and the United Kingdom where anti-Semitism is quickly intensifying, but also from the rest of Europe, Australia, South Africa, China and the whole Western Hemisphere. They will come from every nation on the earth where they have been living. *"A highway will be there"* (Isaiah 35:8) for the Lord's people to go *"home."* The nations will no longer be able to ignore this *"banner."*

Father, we pray that You will help Your Church and yes, even the nations, see this *"banner"* and pay attention to this ensign signaling this great work that You are about in our day. Truly, *"You have given a **banner** to those who fear you, that it may be displayed because of the truth."* (Psalm 60:4 NKJV)

PERSONAL REFLECTION

Gathered, Then Transformed

*"For **I will** take you from among the nations;*
gather you out of all the countries
and bring you into your own land.
***Then I will** sprinkle clean water on you*
and you shall be clean;
***I will** cleanse you from all your filthiness and*
from all your idols.
***I will** give you a new heart and put*
a new spirit within you;
***I will** take the heart of stone out of your flesh*
and give you a heart of flesh.
***I will** put My Spirit within you."*

(EZEKIEL 36:24-27, NKJV)

Many Scriptures echo and confirm this passage from Ezekiel – that the Lord's regathering of His people and His "cleansing" of them is a two-step process. For the majority of Jewish people, the cleansing will occur after they have been gathered back to their land.

Yes, throughout the world today, Jews are coming to Jesus. They are experiencing His forgiveness and cleansing. Messianic congregations are springing up in many nations as well as in Israel. They are the first fruits – the promise of more to come.

We are witnessing an outworking of the Lord's purposes at this moment in history that will include the fulfillment of all the Scriptures that promise forgiveness and cleansing throughout the nation of Israel.

Let us look at a few more passages to see again the Lord's great heart for this people He loves with an everlasting love. His desire is to forgive them.

"I have seen their (rebellious) ways, and I will heal them;
I will lead them and give comfort to them." (Isaiah 57:18 CJB)

Consider this promise from the famous chapter of the valley of dry bones, Ezekiel 37.

v. 23 *"I **will** save them from all their sinful backsliding, and I **will** cleanse them. They will be my people and I **will** be their God."*

v. 28 *"'Then the nations will know that I the Lord **make Israel holy**, when my sanctuary (or home) is among them forever.'"*

Notice all the "I wills" in the Scriptures we are studying today. God intends to move in a visible and sovereign way. The result will be that the Gentile nations will be so aware of His forgiveness for Israel that they will have to acknowledge His Lordship.

Sovereign Lord, we bow before Your throne as we catch glimpses in the Scriptures we are studying of Your plan to gather, forgive and cleanse Your Jewish people. How amazing You are and how all-encompassing are Your purposes on the earth!

PERSONAL REFLECTION

At this point I would like to make an additional comment about a wonderful extra benefit for the Church. When Jewish people accept Jesus as their Messiah and walk with Him, there is often a great depth in their understanding of the Gospel and the Word of God. The Church has made the Christian faith very Gentile. Jewish believers bring us a whole new Scriptural perspective because of their deeper understanding of the Old Testament and how it applies to the New. The Bride of Christ will not be complete without our Jewish brothers and sisters.

Promises Of Forgiveness And Washing

"I will pardon all their sins through which they offended and rebelled against me." (JEREMIAH 33:8, CJB)

This topic of the Lord's cleansing and forgiveness of the nation of Israel is so vital that we need to examine a number of additional Scriptures describing His intent. There are so many promises. Romans 11:26 & 27 states that God's forgiveness of His Jewish people is part of His covenant with them.

> *"The Deliverer will come from Zion;*
> *he will turn godlessness from Jacob. (Israel)*
> *And this is **my covenant** with them*
> *when **I take away their sins**."*

Here are other Scriptures from the prophets, Jeremiah, Zechariah, Joel and Micah.

> *"'...they (Israel) will **all** know me from the least of them to the greatest;' declares the Lord. 'For **I will forgive** their wickedness and remember their sins no more.'"* (Jeremiah 31:34)

> *"On that day a fountain will be opened*
> *to the house of David and the inhabitants of Jerusalem,*
> ***to cleanse them from sin and impurity**."* (Zechariah 13:1)

> *"Judah will be inhabited forever*
> *and Jerusalem through all generations.*
> *Their bloodguilt, which I have not pardoned,*
> ***I will pardon**."* (Joel 3:20 & 21)

> *"Who is a God like you, **who pardons sin***
> *and **forgives the transgression** of the remnant of his inheritance?*
> *You do not stay angry forever*
> *but delight to show mercy.*
> *You will again have compassion on us;*
> *you will tread **our sins** underfoot*

*And hurl all **our iniquities** into the depths of the sea.*
You will be true to Jacob,
And show mercy to Abraham,
as you pledged on oath (the covenant)
to our fathers in days long ago." (Micah 7:18-20)

This last passage from Micah is bursting with God's love, His mercy, His forgiveness and His faithfulness to keep covenant. How revealing are all these Scriptures for us as Christians – adding to our understanding of the greatness of His forgiveness for us!

Lord, when we see the magnitude of Your forgiveness – we cry out in awe,

"Who… is like you, O Lord? Who is like you –
majestic in holiness, awesome in glory, working wonders?"
(Exodus 15:11)

"The Lord, the Lord,
the compassionate and gracious God,
slow to anger, abounding in love and faithfulness,
maintaining love to thousands,
*and **forgiving wickedness, rebellion and sin.**"* (Exodus 34:6 & 7)

PERSONAL REFLECTION

I Will No Longer Hide My Face

"I will no longer hide My face from them, for I will pour out My Spirit on the house of Israel, declares the Sovereign Lord." (EZEKIEL 39:29)

Even before we heard Derek Prince speak in Cleveland in 1971 (described on Day 8), my husband and I had been growing spiritually through his teachings. Derek focused on the Word and poured out his life to preach the Gospel, to help Christians grow in their faith and to bring greater understanding of God's heart for Israel. Over the 30 years of our friendship with Derek, we observed a wonderful consistency in his life. He "walked the talk."

So I bring you the following words from Derek Prince with great confidence that what he related in this experience is authentic and reliable:

"One night I awoke at 2:00 a.m. with a strange sense of excitement. As I lay there wondering why I should be so excited, I heard from the heavenly realm, 'You're excited because all heaven is excited and you are sharing their excitement.'

Why should all heaven be excited?

'…All heaven is excited because Jesus is excited…'

Why is Jesus excited?

'Jesus is excited… because He is about to be reconciled with His brothers and sisters – the Jewish people.'

"I thought about Joseph, how he was rejected by his own brothers, sold as a slave into Egypt and there lost his Jewish identity. To his brothers Joseph no longer existed.

"Yet after many years of separation – without any contact between them – God brought Joseph's brothers to Egypt to seek food. At this time Joseph dressed like an Egyptian and spoke Egyptian. He communicated with his brothers in Egyptian through an interpreter.

"They had no inkling who he was. Eventually, Joseph made himself known directly to his brothers. And he wept aloud, and the Egyptians and the house of Pharaoh heard it.

"Today, for the Jewish people, Jesus has lost His Jewish identity. Grudgingly, they acknowledge Him as the 'Gentile Messiah.' **Yet all heaven awaits in awed excitement the moment fast approaching when Jesus will reveal Himself directly and personally to His Jewish brothers and sisters.** As this has become real to me, I share heaven's excitement!" [8] (My emphasis added)

Lord Jesus, we are so grateful for this word you gave Derek. It helps make "that moment fast approaching" more real. We do want to share Your excitement in this event. We want to have Your attitude toward those to whom we owe so much of our faith. We want to love them as You do.

PERSONAL REFLECTION

Life From The Dead

"But if their transgression means riches for the world,
and their loss means riches for the Gentiles,
how much greater riches will their fullness bring!"
For if their rejection is the reconciliation of the world,
*what will their acceptance be but **life from the dead?"***
(ROMANS 11:12 & 15)

Much has been written on the vital eleventh chapter of Romans (including books mentioned in the booklist at the end of this study.) However, we will focus on just a few of Paul's amazing statements in this chapter as he looks ahead to the day when *"the Gentile world enters in its fullness; and ... all Israel will be saved."* (Romans 11:25 & 26 CJB)

We cannot fully comprehend the meaning of phrases like *"all Israel will be saved"* or *"life from the dead."* But we do know that there is a **time of glory** coming – a time of great illumination – as Jesus reveals Himself to the Jewish people and they are *"grafted (back) into their own olive tree."* (Romans 11:24)

This image of the olive tree represents the Jewish, biblical root of our faith. Paul states that the Jews (the branches) were temporarily cut off from their *"olive tree"* by their rejection of Jesus as Messiah. The Gentiles were grafted in from a *"wild olive tree"* to this Jewish base of our faith. The writers of the Old Testament were Jewish, and Jesus Himself was Jewish, as were all of the New Testament writers with the possible exception of Luke and Titus. We Gentiles must not boast! (Romans 11:18)

Let's look at two of the concluding paragraphs of *Our Hands Are Stained with Blood* as Dr. Brown marvels at these amazing Scriptures that we are highlighting.

> "Today there are men and women across the globe who are children of the living God, the spiritual seed of Abraham, joint-heirs with the Messiah, recipients of eternal life, blood-washed, Spirit-filled, consecrated saints *as a result of Israel's transgression.* **How much greater riches will Israel's fullness bring!**

"At this very moment, a continuous stream of praise ascends to heaven in more than 2,500 languages, and angels shout for joy as sinners repent worldwide *as a result of Israel's loss*. **How much greater riches will Israel's fullness bring!**" [9]

Lord, we cannot even comprehend why You have chosen to bring Your purposes to pass in this way. We can only echo Paul's words as he extols Your greatness:

> *"Oh, the depth of the riches*
> *of the wisdom and knowledge of God!*
> *How unsearchable his judgments,*
> *and his paths beyond tracing out!*
> *Who has known the mind of the Lord?*
> *Or who has been his counselor?*
> *Who has ever given to God,*
> *that God should repay him?*
> *For from him and through him and to him are all things.*
> *To him be the glory forever! Amen.* (Romans 11:33-36)

PERSONAL REFLECTION

Hear The Word Of The Lord, O Nations (Jeremiah 31:10)

DAY 23

*"Come near, you nations, and **listen;***
***pay attention**, you peoples!*
*Let the earth **hear**, and all that is in it,*
...The Lord is angry with all nations;
...For the Lord has a day of vengeance,
a year of retribution, to uphold Zion's cause.
(ISAIAH 34:1, 2 & 8)

In earlier studies, we have seen that the restoration of Israel is *"a sign"* to the nations. Today we will see that the Lord goes even further in His call to the nations of the earth to listen and pay heed to what He is planning.

> *"This is the plan determined for the whole world;*
> *this is the hand stretched out over all nations.*
> *For the Lord Almighty has purposed, and who can thwart him?*
> *His hand is stretched out and who can turn it back?"*
> ***"The Lord has established Zion,***
> *and in her (Zion) his afflicted people will find refuge."* (Isaiah 14:26,
> 27 & 32)

In today's world, we do not yet see Zion as a place of complete refuge and safety. That is still coming. It is promised!

But we do see here a master plan that will not be thwarted by even the most rebellious nation. The Lord has purposed to establish Zion and restore the Jewish people to their covenant land. He has set a plumb line in our midst. The nations are required by God Almighty to make a choice to either align with His purposes or suffer the consequences.

Before the tsunami that swept across the Indian Ocean in late 2004, a Japanese American Christian wrote a book, *God's Tsunami – Understanding Israel and End-time Prophecy*. In it the author, Peter Tsukahira, declares:

"God is not frustrated by human brutality or the cynicism of modern politics. His purposes are still being accomplished in spite of rampant terrorism. He is using tiny Israel to draw a "line in the sand" and draw all peoples into a valley of decision…. He is requiring the world to make a decision regarding who He is and what He has said in His Word, the Bible. As in the days of old Israel is again God's instrument, His lever to shake the nations…the modern evidence of God's covenant faithfulness." [10]

Lord, we tremble for the nations, as we read the Word that states:

"In those days and at that time,
when I restore the fortunes of Judah and Jerusalem,
I will gather all nations
and bring them down to the valley of Jehoshaphat. (meaning God judges)
There I will enter into judgment against them
concerning my inheritance, my people Israel,
for they (the nations) scattered my people
…and divided up my land!" (Joel 3:1 & 2)

Have mercy on our nations, Lord, and help us stand with Your people, Israel. May our commitment not diminish even when Israelis make unwise decisions, even when they still reject the One we hold most dear. We stand with them **for Your Word's sake.**

PERSONAL REFLECTION

Who Is On The Lord's Side?

"For whoever touches (or injures) you touches the apple (or pupil) of His eye." (ZECHARIAH 2:8)

A pastor of an Israeli assembly tells the following story of an amazing change of heart. One night during the 1967 war between Israel and Egypt, an Egyptian soldier was wandering alone in the desert when he saw a light coming toward him. He realized Jesus was revealing Himself. His life was instantly transformed, and soon he became a pastor. But because of bitterness toward Israel, he would not read the Old Testament. In the Yom Kippur War of 1973, he again fought in the Egyptian army against Israel. One day the Lord spoke to him saying: "If you don't love My people Israel, you don't love Me." Forgiven by the Lord and forgiving the Jews, this Egyptian is now teaching his Bible school students "that God still has a covenant with the Jews and the land of Israel is their inheritance." [11]

From our study on Day 23, we see that the Lord is requiring a choice. Who will bless *"one of the least of these brothers of mine"*? (Matthew 25:40) Will we be like the older brother in the story of the Prodigal Son, who enjoyed all his father's riches but refused to accept the return of his lost brother? Or, will we stand with the father, eagerly watching the road for a sign of his return?

The great London preacher and evangelist of the 1800s, Charles Haddon Spurgeon, had this to say on this issue 100 years before the birth of the state of Israel:

> "I think we do not attach enough importance to the restoration of the Jews... But certainly, if there is anything promised in the Bible it is this...The day shall yet come when the Jews, who were the first apostles to the Gentiles, the first missionaries to us who were afar off, shall be gathered in again.

"Until that shall be, the fullness of the church's glory can never come. Matchless benefits to the world are bound up with the restoration of Israel, their gathering shall be as life from the dead."

As the nations have a responsibility to decide how they will treat Israel, so does the Body of Christ, His own Bride, bought with His blood. Each church fellowship must decide! Each pastor! Each family! Each individual! *"Who is on the Lord's side?"* (Exodus: 32:26 KJV)

Dear Lord, You have been showing us through Your Word how important Israel was and is to You. We do not want to injure the *"apple of (Your) eye."* We choose to stand with You. We desire to be on Your side, as You show the Church Your heart and Your purposes toward this nation You call *"My inheritance."*

PERSONAL REFLECTION

May We Be Like Ruth!

"For Zion's sake I will not keep silent,
for Jerusalem's sake I will not remain quiet,
till her righteousness shines out like the dawn,
her salvation like a blazing torch." (ISAIAH 62: 1)

DAY 25

The book of Ruth is not only a wonderful heart-warming story, it is also a prophetic picture with application for today. We could say that the elderly widow, Naomi, returning to Israel is a type of the Jewish people coming "home" from the nations. The two Gentile daughters-in-law, Orpah and Ruth, represent the two diametrically opposite attitudes in the Church.

Orpah decides to leave Naomi and return to her Gentile people to pursue her own life, security and happiness. An extreme example of how this attitude has played out in church history would be an incident in WWII Germany when trainloads of Jews, packed into cattle cars and crying out for help, passed close to a church's window. The church's reaction was to sing louder to drown out their cries. In Matthew 25:45 Jesus comments that what we fail to do for the least of His brethren is what we refuse to do for Him. Doing nothing is not acceptable to Him.

Ruth, on the other hand, decides to throw in her lot with Naomi, to serve and protect her. Her reward is great – even to becoming the great-grandmother of David and a Gentile in the bloodline of Jesus, the Messiah. Ruth represents the part of the Church that is willing to go out of its way to bless the Jewish people and to help them fulfill their divine call to return to their land and to their God.

How do we stand with the Lord and His purposes for Israel today?

First, become informed. There are many excellent resources now available.

Second, counter biased news with the Scriptural point of view. Study the Prophets in the Old Testament. As someone has said, the Lord did not have a "brain scrub" between the Old and New Testament. He is the same! He speaks of judgment in the New as well as the Old. As we have seen, He speaks of mercy throughout both the Old and the New.

Third, assure Jewish friends and neighbors that we, Christians, are standing with them and with Israel in these days when hatred toward Jews is again rising sharply.

Fourth, support Christian groups assisting the Jews to make aliyah and those blessing them once they arrive in the land, by prayer, volunteering, or finances.

Fifth, and of greatest importance, pray for the fulfillment of the Lord's plan in the whole situation in the Middle East. I like to pray the Scriptures, many of which are scattered through this devotional. Then I know I'm not putting my "spin," expectations, or timetable on what the Lord will do. I'm just affirming that what He says in His Word He will do. So I take different Scriptures that the Lord seems to highlight, and I proclaim them out loud. There is great power released when we speak God's Word out into the atmosphere!

Lord, may we be those who cry out to You *"for Zion's sake"* until You fulfill all that You have said You would do. May we be like Ruth and be willing to serve this people even as the world becomes increasingly hostile to them.

PERSONAL REFLECTION

Days Of Grace

*"As long as it is day, we must do **the work** of him (the Father) who sent me (Jesus.) Night is coming, when no one can work."* (JOHN 9:4)

DAY 26

We are living in days of grace! Even as we see the storm clouds gather, we are aware of the tremendous opportunities the Lord is providing for the spread of His Kingdom – to reach unreached peoples and closed-door nations.

We see the Lord intentionally stirring His Bride, the Church, to new life and wooing us closer to His side through a deeper intimacy with Him.

Then there is "the work" we have been discussing – the Lord drawing His Jewish people home to their land to experience His restoration.

In Acts 3:21, Peter makes a significant declaration to the Jews who assemble after the healing of the cripple at the gate of the temple.

"He (Jesus) must remain in heaven until the time comes for God to restore everything, as He promised long ago through His holy prophets."

He, now, is in that process of the *"restoration of all things"*! (NKJV for *"restore everything"*) Yet there is a dark time coming for Israel and all nations. Jesus speaks of it in Matthew 24, Luke 21 and Mark 13. He warns us to be alert and watchful.

Let us reflect on Jeremiah 16:16. *"'But now I will send for many fishermen,' declares the Lord, 'and they will catch them. After that I will send for many hunters, and they will hunt them down on every mountain and hill and from the crevices of the rocks.'"*

As Jesus referred to His disciples as "fishers of men," (Mark 1:17) many involved with aliyah interpret this Scripture to mean that we are also fishermen helping the Jews return home safely where they will meet their Messiah. Sadly, there will also be a day soon when we will not be allowed into certain nations, and the *"hunters"* will suddenly descend upon the Jewish people. This is the compelling reason for the urgency we feel to work quickly to help them home *"while it is day."* (John 9:4 NKJV)

All this is preparation for the Lord's return. So in the last four days of our study together let us focus our thoughts on **His glorious coming**. This joyful expectancy will sustain and encourage us *"so that when the day of evil comes, (we) may be able to stand (our) ground."* (Ephesians 6:13)

The Lord Jesus Himself urges, *"Now when these things* (worldwide troubles) *begin to happen, look up and lift up your heads, because your redemption draws near."* (Luke 21:28 NKJV)

Father, thank You that when everything in Your Word is fulfilled, You will send our Lord Jesus back to this earth. Help us to work diligently in these days of grace that You are giving us before the difficult times come. Then, help us to stand fast in the coming days of darkness, looking to You, *"the author and finisher of our faith."* (Hebrews 12:2 NKJV)

PERSONAL REFLECTION

That Great Day

"They will see the Son of Man coming on the clouds of the sky, with power and great glory." (MATTHEW 24:30)

DAY 27

"For the Lord himself will come down from heaven, with a loud command, with the voice of the archangel, and with the trumpet call of God." (I THESSALONIANS 4:16)

Many of us in the Church are very familiar with these glorious Scriptures in the New Testament. We are those who *"have longed for his appearing"* (II Timothy 4:8) and who are *"looking for and hastening the coming of the day of God."* (II Peter 3:12 NKJV)

Let us take time to ponder and prayerfully consider some of the Old Testament Scriptures that not only tell of His return but also describe how it will affect His people, Israel. Let us also note that the Lord Jesus returns to Zion (Jerusalem), not to London, New York, or Tokyo.

*"When the **Lord returns to Zion**,*
they (Israelis) will see it with their own eyes."
*"Therefore **my people** will know my name;*
...in that day they will know
that it is I who foretold it.
Yes, it is I." (Isaiah 52:8 & 6)

"Then the Lord will go out and fight against those nations, (coming against Jerusalem)...
On that day his feet will stand on the Mount of Olives, east of Jerusalem,
and the Mount of Olives will be split in two...forming a great valley.
...You (Israelis) will flee by my mountain valley, (way of escape from their enemies)
*Then the Lord my God **will come**, and all the holy ones with him."*
(Zechariah 14:3-5)

*"For the Lord will rebuild Zion and **appear in his glory!**"* (Psalm 102:16)

"the Lord will be your everlasting light,
and your days of sorrow will end.
Then will all your people (Jews) be righteous
and they will possess the land forever.
They are...the work of my hands,
For the display of my splendor." (Isaiah 60:20 & 21)

How will His return affect Israel? Look at what we've just read:

They will know His Name.

They will know He foretold His coming.

He will provide a way of escape for them as He stands on the Mount of Olives.

He will be their everlasting light.

The days of their sorrow will end.

They'll all be righteous (forgiven) – for the sake of His Glory or splendor.

They will possess the land forever!

Lord Jesus, we know that Your return will be the climax of history for **Your Church**. Thank You that it will also be the culmination for **Your people, Israel.** Show us how to hasten **that great day!**

PERSONAL REFLECTION

More Promises To Be Fulfilled

*"As you have been an object of cursing among the nations, O Judah and Israel, so will I save you, and **you will be a blessing."** (ZECHARIAH 8:13)

DAY 28

*"I will give them (Israel) **praise and honor in every land where they were put to shame."** (ZEPHANIAH 3:19)

There are many wonderful promises made to Israel that we in the Church have adopted for ourselves down through the ages. These passages have been incredibly life-giving sources of strength to us in our walk with the Lord.

However, some of these same Scriptures fit even better when applied literally to Israel at the end of the age and at the time when the Lord Jesus sets up His visible Kingdom here on the earth. Let us ponder and apprehend what the following Scriptures declare that He has planned for His people Israel!

*"They will sparkle **in his land** like jewels in a crown."* (Zechariah 9:16)

*"You (Israel) will be **a crown of splendor... a royal diadem in the hand of God.**
No longer will they call you Deserted,
Or name **your land** Desolate.
But you will be called Hephzibah, **(My delight is in her)**
and your land Beulah; **(married)**
for the Lord will take delight in you,
...so will your God rejoice over you."* (Isaiah 62:3-5)

*"for the Lord Almighty **will reign
on Mount Zion and in Jerusalem,**
and before its (Jerusalem's) elders, **gloriously."*** (Isaiah 24:23)

*"I will grant salvation to Zion, **my splendor to Israel."*** (Isaiah 46:13)

*"They will be called **the Holy People,
The Redeemed of the Lord;"*** (Isaiah 62:12)

We, the Gentile Church, will also be called by these names and partake in this glory as we join together with our Jewish brothers and sisters – Jew and Gentile – *"the one new man."* (Ephesians 2:15) It is probably very evident by now that many in the Church have neglected to give Israel her due place. We have failed to recognize that these verses are direct promises to the Jewish people. May we stand together in faith that the day is coming when Jew and Gentile will be that *"one new man."*

O Lord, great is your faithfulness! We rejoice in what is coming for both the Church and Israel as we make this proclamation of future victory:

> *"Sing, O Daughter of Zion;*
> *shout aloud, O Israel!*
> ***Be glad and rejoice with all your heart,***
> *O Daughter of Jerusalem!*
> *The Lord has taken away your punishment,*
> *he has turned back your enemy.*
> *The Lord, **the King of Israel**, is with you;*
> *never again will you fear any harm.*
> *On that day they will say to Jerusalem,*
> *'Do not fear, O Zion;*
> *do not let your hands hang limp.(in fear)*
> ***The Lord your God is with you,***
> *he is mighty to save.'"* (Zephaniah 3:14-17)

PERSONAL REFLECTION

Jerusalem, City Of The Great King

"The Lord... will again choose Jerusalem."

(ZECHARIAH 2:12)

DAY 29

There are many amazing words written about the destiny of Jerusalem. As we have seen in the last few devotions, it is often helpful to isolate certain Scriptures on a specific theme or word, in order to see more clearly their importance. So without a lot of commentary, I set out what the Word says about Jerusalem, the city that Jesus Himself called *"the city of the great King."* (Matthew 5:35) As we read and consider them, let us lift up these Scriptures as prayers and proclamations to the Lord.

> *"Afterward you will be called the City of Righteousness, The Faithful City."* (Isaiah 1:26)

> *"...your eyes will see Jerusalem, a peaceful abode, a tent that will not be moved; ...There (in Jerusalem) the Lord will be our Mighty One."* (Isaiah 33:20 & 21)

> *"...all who despise you will bow down at your feet and will call you the City of the Lord, Zion of the Holy One of Israel. ...Although you have been forsaken and hated, ...I will make you the everlasting pride and the joy of all generations."* (Isaiah 60:14 & 15)

> *"At that time they will call Jerusalem The Throne of the Lord, and all nations will gather in Jerusalem to honor the name of the Lord."* (Jeremiah 3:17)

> *"'Then this city will bring me renown, joy, praise and honor before all the nations on earth that hear of all the good things I do for it;*

and they (the nations) will be in awe and will tremble
at the abundant prosperity and peace I provide for it.'" (Jeremiah 33:9)

"And the name of the city from that time on will be:
The Lord is THERE." (Ezekiel 48:35)

"This is what the Lord Almighty says:
'I am very jealous for Zion;
I am burning with jealousy for her.'"
...**"I will return to Zion and dwell in Jerusalem.**
Then Jerusalem will be called **the City of Truth,**
and the mountain of the Lord Almighty
will be called **the Holy Mountain."** (Zechariah 8:2&3)

Lord Almighty, how wondrous is Your plan for this city that You have chosen as **Your** *"resting place for ever and ever"*...where **You** *"will sit enthroned."* (Psalm 132:13 &14) May Your coming, visible Kingdom soon be a reality on this war-torn earth! Until then we will keep praying:

"For Zion's sake I will not keep silent,
for Jerusalem's sake I will not remain quiet,
till her righteousness shines out like the dawn,
her salvation like a blazing torch." (Isaiah 62:1)

PERSONAL REFLECTION

God Will Glorify His Great Name

*"'I will make known my holy name **among my people Israel**.*

I will no longer let my holy name be profaned,
*and **the nations will know that I the Lord am the Holy One in Israel**.*

*...I will display **my glory** among the nations."*

(EZEKIEL 39:7& 21)

On this, our last day together, let us again soak in the Word – in Scriptures that lift us beyond ourselves to catch a vision of His coming Glory! Let us proclaim them, declaring what the Lord will bring to pass. And may these glorious passages from the Word of God minister Life to you now, and until He returns!

*"Your eyes will see **the king** in his beauty."* (Isaiah 33:17)

*"And **the glory of the Lord** will be revealed,*
*and **all mankind together will see it**.*
For the mouth of the Lord has spoken." (Isaiah 40:5)

"They raise their voices, they shout for joy;
*from the west they acclaim **the Lord's majesty**.*
*Therefore in the east give **glory to the Lord**;*
*exalt **the name of the Lord, the God of Israel**,*
in the islands of the sea." (Isaiah 24:14 & 15)

What a picture of worldwide rejoicing! And it concludes in verse 16:

"From the ends of the earth we hear singing:
*'**Glory to the Righteous One**.'"*

Let us join this worldwide throng in glorifying

The "King of Kings and Lord of Lords." (Revelation 19:16)

Let us sing *"the song of Moses, the servant of God, and the song of the Lamb:*

"Great and marvelous are your deeds,
   Lord God Almighty.
   Just and true are your ways,
   King of the ages.
   Who will not fear you, O Lord,
   *and bring **glory to your name?***
   *For you alone are **holy.***
   All nations will come
   and worship before you,
   for your righteous acts have been revealed." (Revelation 15:3 & 4)

*"**Amen. Come, Lord Jesus.**"* (Revelation 22:20)

PERSONAL REFLECTION

{ ENDNOTES }

DAY 5

(1) Anti-Semitism: Defined as feelings of hostility or discrimination toward Jews. This hatred began very soon after Abraham and has continued through the centuries among Gentiles (non-Jews).

DAY 6

(2) Dr. Michael Brown, *Our Hands Are Stained with Blood, the Tragic Story of the "Church" and the Jewish People.* C. Shippensburg, PA: Destiny Image Publishers, 1992, p. 21

DAY 9

(3) Palestine was the name given to Israel when the Romans finally fully conquered it in 135 A.D. It is a derivation of Philistia. The name Israel was used until that time and since 1948.

(4) Norman Grubb, *Rees Howells Intercessor.* United Kingdom: Lutterworth Press, 1952, and Fort Washington, PA by CLC Publications, 1980, p. 229

(5) Ibid. pp. 229 & 230

(6) There were a few years in the second century B.C., following the Maccabeean revolt (celebrated during Hanukah), when Jerusalem was ruled by the Jews.

DAY 17

(7) Canaan was the name of the land of Israel before the Lord led His people into it during the time of Joshua. It is often used as a symbol of the "Promised Land."

DAY 21

(8) Quoted "from the desk of Derek Prince" in Volume One, Issue 4, of "Proclamation – Reaching and Teaching the Whole Earth with the Gospel of God's Kingdom," a publication of:
Derek Prince Ministries-International, PO Box 1950, Charlotte, NC 28219-9501

DAY 22

(9) Dr. Michael Brown, *Our Hands are Stained with Blood, the Tragic Story of the "Church" and the Jewish People* C. Shippensburg, PA: Destiny Image Publishers, 1992, pp. 169 &170

DAY 23

(10) Peter Tsukahira, *God's Tsunami – Understanding Israel and End-time Prophecy.* Self-published in Israel, 2003, p. 6

DAY 24

(11) David Davis, *The Elijah Legacy – The Prophetic Significance for Israel, Islam and the Church in the Last Day.* Self- published in Israel, 2003, p. 242

{ FOR FURTHER STUDY }

BOOKS
Old Testament Prophets: Isaiah through Malachi

Arthur, Kay, *Israel, My Beloved*. Eugene, OR: Harvest House, 1996
The author calls this novel "An historic epic...crossing the borders of time"
We follow a single character, representing Israel, from the time of Jeremiah
until the Lord's return. Very powerful!

Brown, Dr. Michael, *Our Hands Are Stained with Blood, the Tragic
Story of the "Church" and the Jewish People.*
Shippensburg, PA: Destiny Image Publishers, 1992
A sad history of the treatment of the Jewish people throughout Christian
history right up to the present. The wonderful chapter referred to on Day 6
gives the account of Christians who have stood with their Jewish brothers
and sisters.
Website: www.destinyimage.com
Available: Amazon.com

Davis, David, *The Elijah Legacy – The Prophetic Significance for Israel,
Islam and the Church in the Last Days.* Self Published in Israel, 2003
A very insightful Scriptural study of the prophets Elijah and Elisha, with
many present-day stories and facts regarding Israel's current situation from
the perspective of a pastor in Haifa, Israel.
Available: The Galilee Experience – 1-888-838-7928

Gruber, Dan, *The Church and the Jews: the Biblical Relationship.*
Hagerstown MD: Serenity Books, 1997
A scholarly work on the New Testament relationship between Israel and
the Church. I found it very well worth studying. It explains how early in its
history the Church developed its anti-Judaic stance.
Available: Amazon.com

Diprose, Ronald E., *Israel and the Church: The Origin and Effects of Replacement Theology*. Rome, Italy: Instituto Bilbico Evangelico Italiano, 2004

A serious theological examination of the effects of the Church's doctrine of Replacement Theology on the Jewish people.

Available: Christian Friends of Israel Communications, PO Box 2687, Eastbourne, E Sussex, BN22 7LZ, email: info@cfi.org.uk.
PH: 01322 410810

Finto, Don, *Your People Shall Be My People: How Israel, the Jews and the Christian Church will Come Together in the Last Days.*
Ventura, CA: Regal Books, 2001

A very readable explanation of many of the aspects of God's purposes for the Jewish people in our day.

Available: The Caleb Company, 68 Music Square East, Nashville, TN 37203
www.calebcompany.com

Facius, Johannes, *Hastening the Coming of the Messiah*. Tonbridge, Kent, England: Sovereign World Ltd, 2001

A much fuller study of many of the Scriptures in this devotional. Easily read.

Available: Intercessors for America, PO Box 915, Purcellville, VA 20134
www.ifabooks.com or ph: 1-800-872-7729.

Gilbert, Sir Martin, *From the Ends of the Earth – the Jews in the Twentieth Century*. London, United Kingdom: Cassell & Co, 2001

With 400 photographs, this beautiful book is called "an enduring and definitive record of Jewish life in the 20th century" by the biographer of Winston Churchill.

Hayford, Jack, *Why Stand With Israel Today?*
Living Way Ministries, 2002

This excellent eight-page booklet is full of good reasons for standing with Israel in today's world. Very clear and concise.

Available: Living Way Ministries, 14820 Sherman Way, Van Nuys, CA 91405. ph: 1-800-776-8180

Johnson, Paul, *A History of the Jews.*
New York, NY: Harper & Row, 1988
For history lovers. This national best seller covers 4,000 years of Jewish history with an amazing blend of empathy and reality from the point of view of a well-known British historian.

Prince, Derek, *Promised Land: the Future of Israel Revealed in Prophecy.*
Grand Rapids, MI, 2005
Today's news headlines and ancient prophets come together around the tiny struggling land of Israel. Very readable and Scripturally centered by one of the greatest Bible teachers of the 20th century.
Available: Intercessors for America, Po Box 915 Purcellville, VA 20134 www.ifabooks.com or phone 1-800-872-7729

Sanchez, Dr. Dell L., *The Last Exodus.*
San Antonio, Texas: A Jubilee Alive Publication, 1998
History and origin of Spanish speaking Jews in the Americas. "This is the true story of the other side of 1492" and of Christopher Columbus.
Available: Preparing the Way Ministries, PO Box 271693, Fort Collins, CO 80527. PTWmin@juno.com. Also available in Spanish

Sanders, Sharon, *Tell the Children.* Self published in Israel
A "picture story" for little eyes, telling of God's love for the Jewish people.
Available: Christian Friends of Israel, PO Box 1813, Jerusalem 91015, Israel www.cfijerusalem.org

Scheller, Gustav, *Operation Exodus: Prophecy Being Fulfilled.*
Tonbridge, Kent, England: Sovereign World Ltd, 1998
The exciting story of the miraculous beginnings of Operation Exodus, Ebenezer Emergency Fund.
  * *Available: in US: Ebenezer Emergency Fund, PO Box 568, Lancaster, NY 14086. info@ebenezer.org or ph: 716-681-6300,*
  * *in UK: Ebenezer Emergency Fund, 5a Poole Rd, Bournemouth, BH2 5QJ. enquiries@ebenezer-ef.org or ph: 01202 294455*

Schlink, M. Basilea, *Israel – My Chosen People*.
Darmstadt, Germany: Kanaan Publications, 2000
Written by the founder of the Evangelical Sisterhood of Mary – a Lutheran order that was founded after a girls' Bible study group learned what their German people had done to the Jews in World War II.
Available: Evangelical Sisterhood of Mary, Canaan in the Desert, 9849 N. 40th St., Phoenix, AZ 85028 or www.kanaan.org.

Telchin, Stan, *Betrayed!* Grand Rapids, MI: Chosen Books, 1981
"How do you feel when you are successful, 50 and Jewish, and your 21-year-old daughter tells you she believes in Jesus?" The author answers this question in a story hard to put down.
Available: Amazon.com

Tsukahira, Peter, *God's Tsunami – Understanding Israel and End-time Prophecy*. Self published in Israel, 2003
A great blend of the Lord's end-time purposes for the Gospel to spread throughout the earth with His restoration of Israel. "A tsunami of revival is racing across the globe."
Available: website address: www.Gods-Tsunami.com
email: info@Gods-Tsunami.com.

VIDEOS and DVDs

"Jerusalem: 'The Covenant City'" by Hugh Kitson, traces past prophetic history of Jerusalem and explores what the Bible has to say about Jerusalem's present and future destiny. Beautiful footage of Israel with part of the narration by Lance Lambert.
Available in VHS or DVD from Intercessors for America's Bookstore – www.ifabooks.com or 1 800-872-7792
Also available in VHS PAL: Christian Friends of Israel, PO Box 1813, Jerusalem 91015, Israel

"The Covenant, The Story of My People" produced by The International Christian Embassy Jerusalem, is a dramatic musical of the Chosen People and their faith in God. It features an international cast of more than 70. Subtitles are available in French, Norwegian, Swedish, German, Russian and Japanese VHS or DVD.
Also available in PAL format in both Video and DVD
Available: Embassy Resources Ltd., PO Box 1192, Jerusalem 91010, Israel

"A Banner for the Nations" by Hugh Kitson, follows Jewish people as they prepare to emigrate from the former Soviet Union, on board the ship heading for the Promised Land, and as they arrive in Haifa, Israel. Features interviews with the families who are happily settled in their homeland.

"Planted in their Land" by Hugh Kitson, answers the frequently asked question, "What happens after they arrive in Israel?"

These last 2 videos/ DVDs are available in NTSC (US format) and PAL format:

* *in US: Ebenezer Emergency Fund, PO Box 568, Lancaster, NY 14086. info@ebenezer-ef.org or ph: 716-681-6300*

* *in UK: Ebenezer Emergency Fund, 5a Poole Rd., Bournemouth, BH25QJ. enquiries@ebenezer-ef.org or ph: 01202 294455*

"The Eternal Purposes of God" by **Lance Lambert**, produced by Christian Friends of Israel, Jerusalem
Available as single videos or as a set of 4 in NTSC (US format) or PAL format from Christian Friends of Israel, PO Box 1813, Jerusalem 91015, Israel

"The Prophets and the Modern State of Israel" by **Lance Lambert**, produced by Christian Friends of Israel, Jerusalem
Available as set of 2 videos in NTSC or PAL. Also available from CFI, Jerusalem (as above)

{ SCRIPTURE INDEX }